Assessing in Sport

ISBN-13: 978-1-902523-76-8
ISBN-10: 1-902523-76-8

sports coach UK is the brand name of The National Coaching Foundation and has been such since April 2001.

sports coach UK
114 Cardigan Road
Headingley
Leeds LS6 3BJ
Tel: 0113-274 4802 Fax: 0113-275 5019
Email: coaching@sportscoachuk.org
Website: www.sportscoachuk.org

Patron: HRH The Princess Royal

Developed from an original text, *Assessing in Sport* (National Coaching Foundation, 1997) by Sheila McQueen and edited by Douglas Bryce, Penny Crisfield and Tony Dallimore.

Authors
Sarah McQuade, Nigel Weare

Editor
Lucy Hyde

Designer
Saima Nazir

Produced on behalf of **sports coach UK** by
Coachwise Business Solutions
Chelsea Close
Off Amberley Road
Armley
Leeds LS12 4HP
Tel: 0113-231 1310 Fax: 0113-231 9606
Email: enquiries@coachwisesolutions.co.uk
Website: www.coachwisesolutions.co.uk

sports coach UK will ensure that it has professional and ethical values
and that all its practices are inclusive and equitable.

050364

Preface

Assessing in Sport has been written for assessors working with any sportspeople being assessed against a set of standards for a qualification or an award. This includes coaches, officials, tutors, groundsmen and crowd control staff.[1]

The resource has been designed to help you explore the role of the assessor, the tools of assessment and the whole assessment process. Once you have completed this resource, you should be able to:

- describe your role and responsibilities as an assessor
- evaluate a range of assessment tools and select the most appropriate ones for specific situations
- explain the principles of assessment
- outline an effective assessment process
- explain why quality assurance is important and what your role is in ensuring quality assurance throughout your assessments
- undertake assessments in your sport.

[1] In the context of this resource, the term *coach* is used to refer to any of the groups of people listed in this paragraph.

How to Use this Resource

This resource has been designed to support your understanding of the principles and practice of assessment.

A number of activities have been included throughout to test your understanding and ability to translate theory into practice. So that these are meaningful and useful, complete each in the context of your sport and your role as an assessor.

At the end of each section, you will find a self-tester to help you consolidate your knowledge and understanding. If you are uncertain about any particular areas, you may find it helpful to go back and reread the appropriate paragraphs.

Key to Symbols used in the text		⇨	See section specified later in the resource for more information
	Activity	⇦	See section specified earlier in the resource for more information
X✓	Answers		Self-tester
	Bring your learning to life		Stop and consider
ⓘ	Important information		Summary

Throughout this resource, the pronouns he, she, him, her and so on are interchangeable and intended to be inclusive of both males and females. It is important in sport, as elsewhere, that both genders have equal status and opportunities.

Although the emphasis of this resource is on coaching, it is aimed at all those who are involved in sports programmes or who want to learn more about the coaching process (eg coaches, leaders, teachers, instructors, development officers, participants, officials, administrators, volunteers, parents/carers, sport scientists, students) and those with responsibility for the organisation of sport (eg national governing bodies, local authorities, centre managers, sports clubs).

Contents

Section One
The Role of the Assessor

1.1 Introduction

You may be assessing coaches, officials, tutors, or even other assessors. In all these cases, you will be working against at least two, or possibly three, sets of agreed standards:

1 The coach you are assessing needs to meet set standards (National Occupational Standards for Coaching, Teaching and Instructing – NOS CTI).

2 As an assessor, you need to meet certain standards yourself (NOS Learning and Development).

3 The relevant awarding body may also establish standards that need to be met for documentation and accreditation.

1.2 Learning Outcomes

By the end of this section, you should be able to explain:

* your role as an assessor
* the qualities of a good assessor.

ACTIVITY 1 – Your role as an assessor

Before undertaking any assessments, it is important to know who you are assessing, what standards you are assessing them against and who you are undertaking the assessment for. Completing the following activity should help you identify this. You should try and remember to do this before each assessment you undertake. Circle the role you plan to take on and the standards you think you will need to be aware of:

My role:	I will be working against the following standards:	I will be assessing the following people:	I will be assessing against the following standards:	The awarding body is:
Assessor Senior assessor Internal verifier External verifier Senior tutor Senior official Senior referee Senior umpire Other	NOS for Coaching, Teaching and Instructing National governing body standards Assessor standards Verifier standards Other	Coaches Officials Assessors Tutors Ground staff Other	Coaching standards Tutoring standards Assessor standards Awarding body standards National governing body standards Codes of ethics Rules of the game Other	Chartered Institute of Professional Development (CIPD) City & Guilds (C&G) EdExcel (OCR) 1st4sport Qualifications National governing body Other

I will be qualifying for the following assessor qualification:	I will be assessing people for the following qualifications:
A1　　A2　　V1　　V2 Introduction to Assessment Practice in Sport (IAPS) National governing body assessor award Other	

1.3 Responsibilities

A qualification is often a licence to practice. You are responsible for ensuring and maintaining the high coaching standards your participants expect, so your decision to award anyone a licence to practice is very significant.

As an assessor your responsibilities are to:

- **the coaches you assess** – to ensure they are ready for assessment and that your assessment is fair, valid and reliable

- **your national governing body (NGB)** – to monitor and assess the skills which are required to ensure quality coaching and better performance

- **the coaching scheme as a whole** – to maintain, raise and quality assure standards of coaching

- **yourself** – to establish your credibility and reputation through the way you assess.

Section Four

1.4 Benefits

Awarding a qualification to the right person in the right way gives benefits to:

- **the coaches you assess** – who will see you as a source of help and advice in their development and as someone else who is acknowledging their skills, knowledge and understanding

- **your NGB** – you are the trusted linchpin in making assessment work for your sport

- **the coaching scheme (and indeed the profession) as a whole** – you decide whether the person being assessed has the competence required to be awarded a vocational coaching qualification or competence-based coaching award

- **you yourself** – you stand to gain the respect and status due to you as an assessor; recognition that you are good at what you do and offer highly-valued opinions

- **other coaches the qualification-holder comes into contact with** – who view the quality of sport as a result of the decisions you have made

- **to parents and spectators** – who can trust the qualification given.

1.5 Qualities of an Assessor

What sort of person makes an effective assessor? Consider whether you would model yourself on any of the following characters.

Assessor 1

'Right, you're going to be assessed. If you do it wrong, you'll be on hospital food for weeks!'

Assessor 2

'It's just a little assessment. Nothing to take too seriously. After all, you're a capable person, but we have to go through this nonsense.'

Assessor 3

'Over the next week or so, I shall be observing your performance with a view to formal assessment. This will be forwarded to the appropriate approved centre, recommending that the awarding body acknowledge your achievement, or not, as the case may be.

Everyone has their own way of dealing with candidates, but there are some things that should and should not be done when carrying out assessment.

ACTIVITY 2 – Qualities and characteristics of an assessor

Look again at each assessor's comments and jot down two things you feel they could improve on in what they are doing or saying. Identify how this could be improved.

Assessor 1

Assessor 2

Assessor 3

⇨ **Now go to Appendix A, page 75**

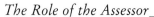
Even though these assessors may not have created the best environment, things can be learned from their example. If you correct their key mistakes, you will find that good assessors:

- create an environment in which assessment is non-threatening and an integral part of the coach's learning experience
- negotiate and communicate with coaches about who is being assessed
- effectively prepare those being assessed
- explain what will happen in clear and simple terms
- are sympathetic and approachable and let those being assessed know they can ask about anything they don't understand
- take the assessment seriously and assess in a systematic and trusted way
- show no favouritism and are fair
- respect each candidate and do not exercise authority (*pull rank*)
- know their stuff.

Realistically, these qualities are not dissimilar to those of a good coach, official or tutor.

1.6 Summary

As an assessor, you are responsible for maintaining the quality standards of the individual you are assessing. You are effectively giving them a licence to practice.

The quality of assessment has a direct impact on the quality of sport. A good assessor has, and makes use of, various qualities and skills to ensure good assessment practice. In this section, you have considered:

- negotiation
- sympathy
- a positive but serious approach
- approachability
- fairness
- respect
- clarity
- knowledge
- a systematic methodology.

1.7 Self-tester 1

1	Consider and outline the role you plan to take on and the standards you think you will need to be aware of:
My role:	
I will be working against the following standards:	
I will be assessing the following types of people:	
I will be assessing against the following standards:	
The awarding body is:	
I will be gaining the following assessor qualification:	
I will be assessing people for the following qualifications:	

---

2 List three types of people who can benefit from good assessment practice. Give one reason why each type benefits:

-

-

-

---

3 List six qualities a good assessor will use when assessing:

-

-

-

-

-

-

Now check your answers in Appendix B. If you had any difficulty, reread the relevant sections. If you are still unsure, contact an assessor or verifier within your national governing body.

Now go to Appendix B, page 93

Section Two

Assessing Coaching Qualifications

2.1 Introduction

Drivers cannot gain their licences without proving their competence to qualified test examiners. Similarly, coaches, officials, tutors and assessors cannot gain their licence to practice without proving their competence to qualified assessors or verifiers. This assessment is usually conducted as part of a vocational coaching qualification or a competence-based coaching award.

2.2 Learning Outcomes

By the end of this section, you should be able to:

- explain what a vocational or competence-based qualification is
- explain which standards you will need to refer to when assessing
- identify units, elements, performance criteria, ranges and evidence specifications.

ACTIVITY 3 – What, how and where

Imagine you are the driving examiner; describe your involvement in the following tasks.

What you will actually do as an assessor.

The main method(s) you will use to conduct the assessment and check competence.

Where you should conduct the assessment.

➡ **Now go to Appendix A, page 76**

2.3 National Standards

Vocational or competence-based qualifications work towards an agreed set of national standards. These may be divided into:

- units, elements and performance or criteria – identifying what needs to be done and what needs to be demonstrated or shown by the coach

- range statements – identifying the different scenarios in which the performance criteria need to be carried out

- evidence specifications – identifying where the assessments should take place, with whom the assessments take place and how many times this needs to be demonstrated.

Table 1 shows an example of what this might look like for someone you are assessing.

Table 1: Sample assessment criteria for a coach

Unit	Element	Performance Criteria	Ranges
Run a session	Organise the group	1 Control the group to maintain safety 2 Organise the group to maximise enjoyment	Environment – indoors/outdoors Group – with beginners/ experienced coach
Evidence Specification	**Both** of the performance criteria. **Three** of the four combined ranges for environment and group.		

Remember that, at the same time as assessing someone else against the standards, you will be working towards a set of criteria for assessors yourself. A simplified example of this may include:

Table 2: Sample assessment criteria[1] for an assessor

Unit	Element	Performance Criteria	Ranges
Assess candidate	Plan assessment	1 Agree areas to be assessed 2 Explain assessment process in terms which the candidate can understand 3 Communicate with others who may be affected	Candidate – experienced/ inexperienced
Evidence Specification	**All** of the performance criteria. **Both** of the ranges of candidate.		

It is important to remember that you are working towards these two separate sets of standards.

Although you are ultimately responsible for your assessment decisions, these may be double-checked by a moderator or verifier to ensure every candidate is assessed by the same standards. You will find more detailed information about this process in Section 6.3.

 Section 6.3

2.4 Summary

In this section, you have considered the following concepts:

• Vocational or competence-based qualifications work to a number of nationally agreed standards.

• Assessors will be using at least two sets of standards when assessing.

• Other people are also involved in assessment, to check the decision-making and quality assure the process. You will find more detailed information about their involvement in Section 6.3.

 Section 6.3

[1] Performance criteria can also be referred to as assessment criteria

2.5 Self-tester 2

I Explain the following terms:

• Elements

• Rangers

• Evidence specifications

---

2 Describe three ways in which you can establish your governing body's standards for the performance criteria.

•

•

•

---

3 Explain how the assessment system makes sure every candidate is assessed by the same standards.

•

Now check your answers with those given in Appendix B. If you had any difficulty, reread the relevant sections. If you are still unsure, contact an assessor or verifier within your NGB.

 Now go to Appendix B, page 94

Section Three

Assessment Methods

3.1 Introduction

There are many methods you can use to determine the competence and knowledge/understanding of the person being assessed. Each method has its strengths and weaknesses.

3.2 Learning Outcomes

By the end of this section, you should be able to:

- describe the strengths/weaknesses of various methods of assessment and explain how they are used in your sport
- outline methods to provide credit for previous learning and experience
- comply with recommendations laid down by awarding bodies such as the Qualifications and Curriculum Authority (QCA), Scottish Qualifications Authority (SQA), 1st4sport Qualifications, City & Guilds (C&G), EdExcel and NGBs of sport in the use of assessments.

3.3 Observation

Observation is a valid method of assessment because it is based on actual performances and uses checklists derived from the performance criteria. However, this doesn't mean it is easy or the only way to assess. You have to know:

- what you are going to assess (precisely what you are looking for)
- exactly what the performance criteria mean
- what is acceptable to your governing or awarding body.

The advantage of observation is that you can actually watch coaches in action with their performers.

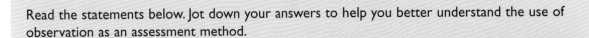

ACTIVITY 4 – Observation

Read the statements below. Jot down your answers to help you better understand the use of observation as an assessment method.

Identify two or three factors that you need to consider to ensure the assessment is valid and reliable. An example is given to help you.

- *Know the standards against which I am assessing inside out.*

Identify any difficulties or limitations in direct observation. An example is given to help you.

- *It may only provide a one-off snapshot of a person's competence*

 Now go to Appendix A, page 77

When gathering evidence against the standards for vocational assessors, you will be expected to demonstrate your competence in observing a candidate. It is highly likely that you will also be monitored or observed while making one of these observations.

During your observation of someone's performance, you will use NGB assessment documentation as well as your own methods of recording your observations.

ACTIVITY 5 – Recording observations

Look at the following methods of recording observations. Consider their strengths and weaknesses, and write down possible solutions to overcome any disadvantages identified.

Method	Advantage	Disadvantage	Possible Solution
National Governing Body Checklist	*Standardised* *Both candidate and assessor know the criteria and paperwork to be used*	*You need to know the paperwork well to navigate it easily while still observing the candidate*	*Familiarisation of paperwork before assessment*
Personal Notes			
Audio Tape			
Video Tape			

 Now go to Appendix A, page 78

3.4 Simulation

Wherever possible, your assessment should be an observation of a real-life example. However, some elements of competence are difficult to assess in *real* or *live* situations, such as assessing the candidates' ability to deal with accidents and emergencies. The chances are that accidents will only occur when no assessor is present. In situations such as these, a simulation exercise, that is, an exercise that mimics real life, could be set up to assess the person's competence. The guiding rule is to make simulations as realistic as possible.

It is best to conduct simulations in the workplace (eg on the pitch, in the gym) but, if this is too difficult to arrange, you could use a different place offering appropriate conditions.

Many NGBs currently use simulation as part of their assessment process to cover a variety of elements of competence.

3.5 Other Assessment Tools

There will be occasions when you will need to use methods other than observation or simulated observation. The next activity provides an opportunity to consider the relative merits of these methods.

ACTIVITY 6 – Other assessment methods

Write down ways other than observation which could help determine whether a person is competent and/or has the specified underpinning knowledge.

Note any obvious strengths or weaknesses of each method in the appropriate column:

Assessment Method	Strengths	Weaknesses

 **Now go to Appendix A, page 79**

Having compared your answers with those offered in the back of this resource, you can review your ideas about strengths and weaknesses as you work through the next few sections.

3.5.1 Projects and Assignments

Projects and assignments are very similar but, generally, the project is a longer piece of work. Of course, both should be as lifelike as possible and relevant to the person's role. An example of an assignment is provided below.

Assignment

Design a fitness programme for a specific performer over a 12-month period, justifying the content of each phase.

What projects and assignments are set in your sport to test a coach's competence and understanding?

3.5.2 Case Studies

A case study usually involves studying one or more performers over a period of time (eg a week, month or season). It might include:

• an analysis of participants' needs and aspirations

• a detailed plan of the coaching session/programme

• a log of how the programme was conducted and modified

• an analysis of the progression, development and performance gains of selected participants

• an evaluation of the programme

• a projection of future work.

This is a useful tool for assessing long-term strategies. An example is given below.

Case Study

Ask three of your performers to complete a food log over a three-day period (including either a Saturday or Sunday).

Analyse their diets in relation to their needs and lifestyles. Discuss the diet with each performer and suggest modifications as required. Set goals with each performer and monitor progress over a four-week period.

The advantages of projects, assignments and case study methods of assessment are that they:

- require coaches to apply knowledge and understanding to real situations

- can be readily tailored to individual sports

- give coaches the opportunity to demonstrate the range and depth of their knowledge and understanding, for which there is rarely time or opportunity through observation.

On the other hand, they:

- may favour those who can write well (rather than those who can perform the role well)

- are open to abuse (eg candidates could fabricate evidence or copy the work of others)

- take time to mark; the marking can be subjective.

What case studies are used in your sport to test a coach's competence and understanding?

3.5.3 Written Questions

Traditionally, exams, short-answer questions and multiple-choice questions have been used by governing bodies to test coaches. The major advantage is they can test underpinning knowledge (ie factual information) and allow the candidate to demonstrate understanding. Exams can be open- or closed-book. In an open-book exam, the candidate is allowed to refer to materials. A closed-book exam is normally conducted in an examination room under examination conditions.

Closed-book exams are usually:

*   a test of memory

*   more stressful to a candidate

*   designed to test what a candidate already knows.

Open-book exams usually:

*   allow a candidate to learn while going through the assessment

*   are less stressful to a candidate

*   test a candidate's ability to find information and use exploratory techniques

*   encourage a candidate to research further.

The multiple-choice format has certain advantages over short- and long-answer questions because it:

*   does not favour those who write well

*   is objective and easily marked

*   is less threatening

*   is less time consuming for both candidates and assessors

*   can be used as a form of assessment in the training environment to identify areas of limited knowledge or understanding.

Its major weaknesses are that:

*   it can sometimes be a test of memory

*   people can guess the right answer (although this can be countered by careful design so that candidates don't know how many responses are correct, or are penalised for wrong answers).

What written questions are used in your sport to test
a coach's competence and understanding?

3.5.4 Evidence from Prior Achievement

Accreditation of Prior Learning (APL) or Accreditation of Prior Achievement (APA)

What about the situation in which someone has been carrying out a role very successfully for a number of years and claims, 'I already do that'? You may be able to accept some evidence of successful past performance as proof of competence. However, this is a difficult area to assess. For instance, should you take people's word about their experience in a particular area?

APL is about the accreditation of prior experience and learning through the assessment of the coach or official's portfolio of evidence against a specific qualification. The following principles need to be considered:

- **identification** – identifying the evidence of experience/learning

- **authenticity** – assuring the evidence and establishing proof

- **currency** – assessing when the experience/learning took place and, consequently, its relevance

- **sufficiency** – estimating whether there is enough evidence

- **validity** – judging the evidence against relevant performance criteria

- **accreditation** – crediting the prior learning towards the award.

APA is accreditation for prior achievement. Primarily, this is used to transfer parts of or a whole qualification from one area of expertise to another, to match qualifications from different awarding bodies or countries. It is also used to determine candidates' readiness to attempt higher levels of qualification.

Assessing APL/APA

If you are confident that the prior achievement or learning of your candidates meets all the criteria, you can credit them with a certain level of readiness for their observed assessment. The important things to remember about APL assessment are that it:

- doesn't need to be linked to a particular education or training programme (eg it can be credited from independent study, practical experience, observations or testimonials from others)

- can be disparate and diverse in nature (eg the sufficiency criteria can be fulfilled by accumulating evidence from a number of different sources)

- is in the control of the learner (ie the individual identifies the experiences).

The area of APL can be very complicated and has led to some confusion. However, what APL really means to the existing coach and assessor is **assessment by portfolio**. In effect, this typically involves:

- identification of evidence by the individual (with or without guidance)

- gathering or generating evidence by the individual (the portfolio)

- assessment of the evidence by the assessor (the portfolio)

- accreditation and recognition of the evidence in the portfolio by the assessor

- guidance provided to the individual by the assessor.

In this way, individuals are encouraged to be self-monitoring, proactive, responsible and accountable for their own development and accreditation. The next activity helps you to think through the sort of evidence which might need to be included in the portfolio.

ACTIVITY 7 – Using APA/APL

Jot down the sort of evidence that would suggest the candidate has previously achieved the following competence criteria. One example has been given to help you.

- *Current NGB coaching awards*

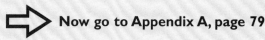 **Now go to Appendix A, page 79**

The most difficult part of this process is advising coaches about which evidence from prior achievements they should select and submit in the portfolio. Many experienced coaches will have logbooks or diaries which document their experience and practice. These may also help to demonstrate their knowledge, understanding and ability, and how they apply this.

At Level 2 of the National Occupational Standards (NOS), most sports expect coaches to have been recently observed in running an appropriate session, whatever APL evidence they might present. At Level 3 and above, much more emphasis is placed on APL.

Assessment of this kind of portfolio is extremely useful in updating and prolonging licences or qualifications. The existing holders can show that they are continuing to function in their role at the same or better level of competence, and that they are up to date.

Are APL and APA used in your sport to test a coach's
competence and understanding? If so, how?

3.5.5 Verbal Questioning

Many of the limitations of assessment methods mentioned so far may be overcome by
asking candidates questions. This allows you to:

- check understanding by asking why they're doing what they are doing

- discuss areas in which you are uncertain about their competence

- examine the knowledge which underpins their performance

- provide additional evidence to support your judgement of their competence

- check competence across a specified range (eg different age groups, genders).

Verbal questioning will be an essential supplement to all forms of assessment. Some
examples of questions are given in Activity 8.

It is preferable, where possible, to use open questions. These allow candidates the
freedom to demonstrate their knowledge and understanding. Open questions are
characterised by words such as *what, how, why* and *where*.

Closed questions usually elicit a *yes* or *no* response, so don't give you a lot of
information. They are most useful for checking things you may have missed, for
clarification or as starter questions, which can then lead on to other open questions.
Closed questions are characterised by expressions such as *are you, did you, would you,
do you*.

When gathering evidence against the standards for vocational assessors, you will be
expected to show you can use standardised national governing body questions as well
as those you have created for a specific assessment situation. All questions and
responses should be recorded as evidence of your competence.

There are inevitably some disadvantages to an overuse of questions. For example,
they could be:

- time consuming

- subjective

- threatening.

3.6 Choosing the Ways to Assess

In conducting assessments of a coach's competence and knowledge/understanding, there is a preferred order for the assessment methods used:

1 **Observation of task and verbal questioning** – where the candidate carries out the role in a realistic situation.

2 **Observation of simulation and verbal questioning** – where the candidate carries out the role in a set-up or contrived situation.

3 **Assessment of project** – where the candidate takes part in an assignment, written test or case study.

Section Five

There is more to assessment than simply watching or observing a coach in action and ticking a checklist. You will have to think about:

• what you are looking for

• how best to identify it

• how to check the knowledge (ie theory) parts of performance.

ACTIVITY 8 – Using questions to support the assessment

Read the following performance criteria and write down, in the middle column, how you think they should be assessed. Include some questions you may wish to ask in the final column.

Performance Criteria	Methods of Assessment	Sample Questions
Participants are physically and mentally prepared to participate	Observation and questioning	*In what other ways could you make sure participants are prepared physically and mentally?*
All communications are clear, accurate and presented in a style appropriate to participants		
Explanations/demonstrations are clear, technically correct and appropriate to participants		

Continued overleaf

Participants are encouraged and motivated throughout the session		
Prior experiences are correctly identified		
Feedback aims to raise the participants' self-esteem and motivation		

Now select one example of each type of assessment you have proposed and give some details. For example, if you have written *case study*, design one case study; if you have written down *observation*, identify some of the items you would include on a checklist. Identify the performance criteria (PC) you are selecting for each:

Outline of case study for _____ (PC):

Example of items on an observation checklist for _____ (PC):

Example of an assignment for _____ (PC):

Sample questions for a multiple choice paper for _____ (PC):

 Now go to Appendix A, page 80

As you put this form of assessment into practice, you will discover that one example of a person's session can cover a whole range of performance criteria, elements and sometimes units. It is not necessary to carry out separate assessments for all the performance criteria.

One of the skills of an assessor is to credit the person being assessed with as much evidence as possible from a single session. For example, if you observe a coach who has been asked to produce a plan and conduct a session using it, the observation will probably produce evidence for two or three units (eg planning a session, running a session, health and safety).

It is important to remember that in an assessment situation, you are assessing the candidate, not the checklists or the qualification. These are tools that help to make the assessment valid and reliable. Provided that sufficient evidence has been generated by candidates during their performance on more than one occasion to show they are competent, there should be no problem in the assessor justifying the decision.

> **In summary:**
>
> • A separate assessment is not required for each performance criteria.
>
> • Vocational or competence-based qualifications are about the assessment of competence in whole work roles.
>
> • There is no correlation between the quality and quantity of assessment evidence.

3.7 Recording the Evidence

Whatever method you use to assess your candidates and check their competence/ knowledge and understanding, it must be directly relevant to the performance/ assessment criteria being assessed. In addition, you will be required to justify your decision about the assessment. To enable you to do this, it is essential to take notes during candidates' performance and to record any questions you asked and the answers provided, either in written or mechanical form (eg audio tape). These will support any governing body checklist you may have to complete.

Your records will be used as part of a verification process internally, and possibly externally, and could be used in the future by the candidate as evidence of APL or APA.

3.8 Summary

In this section, you have looked at different types of assessments, how to use them effectively and how to verify the existing knowledge and experience that coaches or officials may have.

You have considered:

• **what assessment is** – finding out and making judgements which are reliable and valid

• **ways of assessing** – observation, simulation, assignments, projects, written tests, case studies, questioning, APL, APA

• **testing knowledge** – ensuring coaches know why they are doing what they are doing, and how to adapt what they are doing across a wide range of circumstances.

3.9 Self-tester 3

1 Allocate a preferred order to the following methods of assessment for competence-based qualifications (some may have the same number):			
Method	**First Priority**	**Second Priority**	**Third Priority**
Assignments			
Case Studies			
Multiple-choice Questions			
Observation			
Projects			
Simulation			
Questioning			

2 Write down one advantage and one disadvantage of each type of assessment:		
Method	**Advantage**	**Disadvantage**
Case Studies		
Multiple-choice Questions		
Observation		
Questioning		
Simulation		

Assessment Methods

3 Explain what is meant by:

- APL:

- Candidates might provide:

- Criteria:

5 Why is it important to record your decisions clearly?

Now check your answers with those in Appendix B. If you had any difficulty, reread the relevant sections. If you are still unsure, contact an assessor or verifier within your NGB.

 Now go to Appendix B, page 95

29

Section Four

Fair, Valid and Reliable Assessment

4.1 Introduction

Being an assessor is rather like being a combination of detective and judge; your main role is to make fair judgements or decisions based on sound evidence. This means looking for evidence of competence and making judgements about whether or not your candidates are competent enough to qualify for a vocational- or competence-based qualification.

There are good and bad detectives and judges. An assessor who is a good detective and judge will make a fair assessment; that is, one that is valid and reliable.

4.2 Learning Outcomes

By the end of this section, you should be able to explain what is a:

- fair assessment
- valid assessment
- reliable assessment.

Before we consider these terms in more detail, let us identify what is meant by the word *fair*.

ACTIVITY 9 – Fair selection

You have been asked to select a team, crew or squad for a match.

How would you ensure the selection is fair?

What could happen if no criteria are used?

➡ **Now go to Appendix A, page 81**

4.3 Valid Assessment

To be effective, an assessment has to be valid. Is the assessment really judging the coach's ability to coach, the official's ability to officiate, the tutor's ability to provide learning opportunities, or the assessor's ability to carry out reliable and valid assessments?

As an assessor, you have to be able to argue that the decisions you make about a coach's competence are fair and defensible. You must be absolutely sure that your test is the right test. It is more likely to be valid if it takes place in the workplace, such as during a coaching session. In this situation, you can actually observe the coach in action, either in a live situation or one that is simulated using the detailed performance/assessment criteria laid down.

For more information about observation and simulation, see Section 3.4, page 18.

⬅

Section 3.4

It is important to remember that most assessments cannot measure typical performance (ie the usual performance of the person being assessed), because the act of assessing itself changes the situation. It is important, therefore, to make the assessment environment as natural as you can and ensure you are as unobtrusive as possible.

4.4 Reliable Assessment

In everyday use, things are reliable if you can depend on them. You might say your car is reliable if it always starts and gets you where you want to go. Being reliable in assessment terms means being consistent. For example, an assessment would be deemed reliable if the same result is obtained by any other competent assessor or the same standard of performance always produces the same result.

ACTIVITY 10 – Reliable assessment

Think of two or three factors which you need to consider if you are to secure the reliability (consistency) of your assessment.

 Now go to Appendix A, page 81

Now go to Appendix A, page 81

To produce reliable assessments, tests need to be consistent and be repeated. If you carried out the assessment a week or a month later, would you obtain the same results? Would any other assessor using the same criteria ensure the same outcome?

4.5 Summary

In this section, you have looked at the following terms and principles:

- **Assessment** – fair judgement based on good evidence.

- **Reliability** – an assessment is said to have reliability if it results in a decision that can be repeated.

- **Validity** – an assessment is deemed to have validity if it is assessing the candidate's competence in carrying out the role, is fair and defensible, and is assessed against national standards.

4.6 Self-tester 4

1 Explain what is meant by reliability in assessment:
•
•

2 Explain what is meant by validity in assessment:
•
•

3 **It is possible that the person being assessed could be disadvantaged or disabled in some way. Jot down some considerations you would have to make to ensure your assessment is fair.**

4 **Explain how you can ensure the person being assessed can really achieve the performance criteria (ie it is not just a stroke of luck):**

Now check your answers with those given at the back of the resource. If you had any difficulty, reread this section. If you are still unsure, contact an assessor or verifier within your NGB.

 **Now go to Appendix B, page 96**

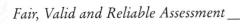

Section Five

The Assessment Process

5.1 Introduction

Now that you have an understanding of the key skills and qualities of an assessor and the principles of fair and reliable assessment, it is important to focus on how to translate this theory into practice that is, how to conduct assessments. This section focuses on conducting assessments using observation and questioning as the primary assessment methods. It explores the processes involved; from preparing for the assessment right through to completing the paperwork and documentation.

5.2 Learning Outcomes

By the end of this section, you should be able to:

- identify the eight phases of the assessment process
- explain the importance of pre-planning an assessment
- prepare yourself and the person being assessed
- carry out each step of an assessment
- explain the importance of keeping accurate records
- report the results of your assessment accurately
- gather the necessary evidence to demonstrate your competence as an assessor, in accordance with agreed standards.

5.3 The Eight Phases

It is helpful to divide the assessment process into eight successive phases:

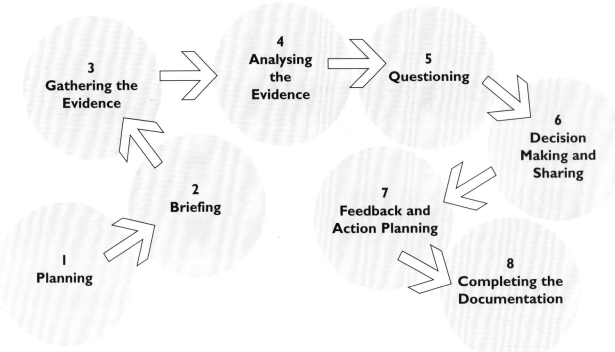

Figure 1: The eight phases of the assessment process

You will need to prove you understand this process and can demonstrate it in action to enable you to be accredited as an assessor. Each step will be considered in a little more detail in the following sub-sections.

5.3.1 Planning

To do any job well, you should be thoroughly prepared. As an assessor, you should reflect on the things to consider when preparing to conduct an assessment.

You will soon realise that good planning and preparation is as important to assessing as it is to coaching, officiating and tutoring. In your planning you will need to consider what:

- is being assessed
- governing body standards exist
- makes up an assessment
- paperwork needs to be prepared
- you know about the coach
- you know about yourself
- facilities need to be prepared
- impact the assessment could have on other people.

Let us now consider these elements in more detail.

What is Being Assessed?

It may sound obvious, but thinking about what is being assessed is crucial. It is important to judge everyone by the same criteria, or the whole system becomes unfair and invalid. Part of your toolkit as an assessor is the checklist of performance/assessment criteria.

Performance/assessment criteria offer a:

- checklist of actions to examine
- personal check that you have covered everything
- way of checking that each task is done properly
- way to identify any task that has not been done properly
- way of accurately judging achievement.

When starting to prepare for assessment, the appropriate criteria need to be identified and agreed with the person being assessed. It is critical that you both know and understand exactly what is being assessed.

Governing Body Standards

Your governing body will expect that all assessors are able to assess consistently to the same standard, regardless of the candidate being assessed, the location in which the assessment takes place and who is conducting it.

In order to be able to undertake this role, you will have to ensure that you:

- are familiar with governing body rules, codes and guidelines
- know and understand the performance/assessment criteria
- know how to use assessment tools in practice (eg observation checklists, session plans, coaching logs). These tools should, if completed satisfactorily, provide all the evidence required to show the candidate is competent
- check whether your governing body has already established how the standards should be interpreted. In most cases, an assessment will have been done before and the procedures agreed
- discuss how performance/assessment criteria are handled with other assessors
- cross-check your findings with your internal verifier.

What Makes Up an Assessment?

It has been suggested that it is best to assess by watching the coach in action, but there are other things to consider when you are observing, such as checking:

- all the correct equipment is available

- you can see and hear clearly and accurately what the person being assessed is doing

- you can assess the candidate without disturbing normal routines too much

- whether you need any colleagues to assist in the assessment.

When you are using simulated situations, check that:

- the situation is as realistic as possible

- a suitable location has been found

- all the correct equipment is available

- other experts are available to assist, if necessary.

When you are using questioning to verify knowledge and understanding, check that your questions:

- take into account any specific needs (eg hearing difficulties)

- are open and searching and not leading (ie cannot be guessed at)

- are clear and unambiguous

- are specific and not general

- are directly relevant to what is being assessed.

When using projects, assignments and case studies, check that:

- they relate directly to the assessment requirement

- the guidelines are clear and unambiguous.

You may be required to produce evidence to demonstrate that you are practising as an assessor. This may include a written assessment plan being agreed with your candidate, detailing the preparation of the assessment.

ACTIVITY 11 – Planning for the assessment

Assume you are going to conduct an assessment on someone in your sport against the performance/assessment criteria opposite using observation, questioning and logbook/portfolio evidence. Plan each stage of the assessment by completing the plan opposite:

Performance/Assessment Criteria:

- Participants are physically and mentally prepared to participate.
- All communications are clear, accurate and presented in a style appropriate to the participants.
- Explanations and demonstrations are clear, technically correct and appropriate to the participants.
- Participants are encouraged and motivated throughout the session.
- Prior experiences are correctly identified.
- Feedback aims to raise the participants' self-esteem and motivation.

General

Sport:	Date:
Time:	Venue:

Level of Award

Number of participants:	Experience of participants:
Age of participants:	

The person being assessed has planned to do the following:

Facility Requirements	Equipment Required
	What equipment does the candidate plan to use?
	What equipment and paperwork do you, the assessor, need?

Significant Others

Who else might be affected by the session?	Who is going to make contact with them?

Briefing

What should the person being assessed produce for you to see before the session begins?	What are you going to need to discuss with the candidate and how should it be recorded?

Session Observation Checklist

Produce a simple checklist which ensures you remember to record evidence against the agreed performance criteria and ranges:

Standard Oral Questions Prepared

What questions might you ask to cover the six performance criteria?

Feedback to Candidate

What three things should you include within your feedback?	How will you record this feedback?

Paperwork

What paperwork will the person being assessed require?	What paperwork should you, the assessor, keep?

 Now go to Appendix A, page 83

Some of these points may be inappropriate on the day of the assessment. For example, if it is the first time the person is being observed, it is unlikely that there will be much evidence to review in the portfolio.

If the person being assessed is experienced, give as much feedback as possible but take away the portfolio for examination to gauge whether the person being assessed is ready for a final assessment and accreditation.

When testing knowledge through oral questioning, you may find it useful to record the interview on audiotape. This will prove invaluable in helping to make objective judgements and the final decision, as well as providing specific evidence. Otherwise, explain to the candidate that you must record the questions on paper, which will take time, and may leave silent gaps.

What Paperwork Needs to be Prepared?

You will need to ensure the appropriate documents are available. These might all be produced by, and specific to, your governing body. You may be assessing the candidate on more than one occasion, so you will need to take notes each time to ensure an accurate assessment. You may devise your own observation prompt sheets, use ready-made national governing body forms or keep records in your diary. Whatever you do, invite the person being assessed to look at your notes, date and sign them. This ensures they are aware of everything that is recorded.

When you first start assessing, you may find it useful to avoid completing forms or writing reports while observing so that you concentrate on the candidate rather than the paperwork. Jot down brief notes, but leave detailed paperwork until after the observation. You will obviously need to allocate more time to the assessment process in order to transfer your notes, and the candidate will need to stay too, to countersign the finalised paperwork. As you become more familiar with the assessment tools, you may find it more time-efficient to write straight onto them.

The paperwork you need for an assessment could include:
- assessor guidance notes
- candidate registration form
- planning contact record
- assessment plan
- observation sheets
- assessment sheets
- question sheets
- answer booklets
- result sheets
- feedback forms
- action planning forms
- summary sheet.

Your governing body may not use all of these, or may combine some. It is important that you become familiar with the paperwork used.

What You Know of the Coach

Think back to when you were observed and tested for your coach or officiating qualification. Perhaps you were nervous and unsure. Maybe you were over-confident and thought there was no way you could fail. Or what about your driving test?

You need to ensure, through careful preparation and discussion, candidates realise that:

- assessment is part of the learning process and you want them to succeed
- credit can be gained for any evidence produced (not just the whole qualification)
- no-one will think them stupid if problems arise
- it is not a once-and-for-all pass/fail situation; it is possible to have any number of attempts.

Remember the object is that candidates have the opportunity to demonstrate they can achieve the performance criteria; you are not trying to fail them.

ACTIVITY 12 – Additional requirements

Some coaches may need special or additional preparation. In the left-hand column below, jot down who you think might be entitled to this. In the right-hand column, write down any additional considerations you would make.

Type of Coach	Additional Requirements

 Now go to Appendix A, page 84

What You Know of Yourself

You know your sport and your job as an assessor. You have all the performance/ assessment criteria before you, have decided how to do the assessment and have thought about the candidate's needs. Now, what about you?

It is only natural to like some people more than others. It is also natural to dislike some people. However, you must be sure you do not let your likes and dislikes cloud your judgement. All you need to know is whether the person being assessed can achieve the performance/assessment criteria. One of the fundamental principles of assessing competence-based qualifications is that there is no discrimination on the grounds of gender, race, creed or age. How could you do a fair assessment if you discriminate on these grounds?

ACTIVITY 13 – Knowing yourself

Here are a few types of candidate or assessor whose personal characteristics could cloud judgement. Explain what you think each means:

Type of Person	Meaning
The *halo effect* candidate	
The *horns effect* candidate	
The *cuddly bunny effect* candidate	
The *perfectionist effect* assessor	

Continued overleaf

The *ruthless executive effect* assessor	
The *hate-to-offend effect* assessor	
The *play-it-safe effect* assessor	

➡ **Now go to Appendix A, page 85**

What Facilities Do You Need to Prepare?

In planning for your assessment, you will need to consider how to create the right environment, ie the facilities you require to conduct all phases of the assessment.

ACTIVITY 14 – Preparing facilities

In the left-hand column below, identify what facilities you will need in order to conduct your assessment. In the right-hand column, identify who would be responsible for organising those facilities.

Facilities	Responsibility

 Now go to Appendix A, page 86

Impact on Others

You have a duty to carry out assessments with minimal disruption to normal activities. The assessments you run can affect a whole host of people, so it is important to consider and communicate with any of the people who might be affected. This can affect the quality of the evidence the person being assessed can produce, as well as implications on health and safety. It can also affect future assessments at the same site.

ACTIVITY 15 – Impact on others

Identify who the assessment may impact on.

Others

 Now go to Appendix A, page 86

You have now completed this important section dealing with preparation. You will find that a number of other issues have also been covered in this section. You may want to use the following checklist to help you in your planning and preparation.

Planning and preparation checklist

Do I:	✓ or X

have the national governing body standards to hand?

know the paperwork and performance/assessment criteria against which I am assessing?

know how to conduct observations, use simulations and questions to allow the candidate to demonstrate their competence?

know that my first impression of a candidate can be affected by all sorts of unimportant considerations?

Have I:

negotiated the planning with the person I am assessing?

prepared the assessment site?

communicated with anyone who might be affected by my assessment practices?

Can I:

take notes during your assessment (do not write the report)?

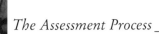

The preparation leads you naturally into the first stage of the assessment – the all-important briefing.

5.3.2 Briefing

It is your duty to make sure that candidates are absolutely clear about what you want them to do. If they are not clear, they could do the wrong things, fail their assessments and gain no credit, even if they are perfectly capable of fulfilling the performance criteria.

How Should You Brief the Candidate?

At the very least, you must be sure that the information you give about the assessment is clear and accurate, which is why you need to prepare. The candidate's agreement of your assessment plan is crucial to making it work.

What Should Your Briefing Contain?

- Cross-check what is to be assessed with the person being assessed.

- Inform the person being assessed about:
  – where the assessment will take place
  – how long it will take.

- Discuss and agree with the person being assessed:
  – the performance criteria
  – the national governing body standards
  – your assessment methods
  – knowledge areas for questions
  – any questions the coach or official may have
  – when the plan will be reviewed.

ACTIVITY 16 – Briefing candidates

How can you check that candidates have understood your briefing? What questions will you ask them? List these in the space below.

 Now go to Appendix A, page 87

Appendix A

You must check every candidate's understanding. Most of the questions suggested in Appendix A on page 87 are closed, but could be used as starter questions. The subsequent discussion can develop from the answers received.

Section Three

If you are not sure about closed and open questions, go back to the sub-sections on questioning, in Section Three.

Based on the checklist you or the governing body have developed and together with the forms of evidence you identified, carry out the briefing as far as you are able. Record the essentials on a written assessment plan, which should be signed by the candidate to confirm understanding and agreement.

Once this is complete, you are ready to move onto the next step in the assessment process: the observation.

5.3.3 Gathering the Evidence

Before you begin to observe and analyse the evidence, you must ensure that you have done a number of things. You must:

- ensure that your observation is structured and that you can see and hear the candidate from a position that does not interfere with what is happening (ie remain unobtrusive). Remember that you will need to observe from different positions as the assessment progresses

- ensure that you have a reliable method for taking notes. The notes should be legible, relevant and easy to record

- ensure that you are familiar with the performance criteria prior to the assessment. Key things to note are:
  - the length of time taken for each task
  - the transitions between them

- check any deviations – are they relevant/necessary?

- record what you observe

- ensure accuracy and detail where appropriate.

5.3.4 Analysing the Evidence

You are now equipped with the tools required to carry out an assessment, you have produced an assessment plan, fully briefed your candidate and are now ready to analyse the coach's evidence using observation and questioning as your tools.

ACTIVITY 17 – Golden rules of observation

In the space below, jot down three or four golden rules you should consider to ensure that your observation is effective.

 Now go to Appendix A, page 87

 In case of doubt about the criteria, the standards or ways to observe, ask someone such as your internal verifier or senior assessor for advice.

So far, you have enabled the person being assessed to produce evidence of competence by:

- observing the candidate *working* as normal
- using an appropriate simulation
- checking their work against the performance criteria
- checking the candidate's portfolio, including the logbook.

If you still do not feel you have enough evidence to make an assessment decision, you may:

- observe the person being assessed again to confirm your views
- set up another version of the same simulation
- ask some more questions
- ask to see assignments and projects
- ask the person being assessed for any further evidence.

If, after this, you are still unsure, you may consult your internal verifier or senior assessor.

Analysing the evidence checklist

Do I:	✓ or X
test for knowledge and understanding by asking questions?	
only test specified knowledge areas?	
if a candidate has difficulty with a question, try to find out why?	
ensure your questions are absolutely clear (check for understanding and restate if necessary)?	
ensure I am aware of a candidate's disadvantages or difficulties and do something about it?	
if in doubt about an assessment, look for further evidence to help make up your mind?	
check the candidate's portfolio containing supplementary evidence?	

5.3.5 Questioning

The assessment is not finished once you have finished observing the candidate. You will need to use questions as an assessment tool to:

- clarify whether they are competent in certain criteria that were not seen or demonstrated during the assessment

- establish what else they know and understand

- how they would progress this activity/session to ensure participants growth and development

- find out what they might do in contrasting scenarios, say with other participants, in different activities/sessions or if accidents and injury should occur.

Your questions should fall within the agreed areas to be assessed and should not be designed to catch people out.

The ability to use a range of questions effectively is an essential part of this phase of the assessment and often improves with practice and experience.

ACTIVITY 18 – Effective questioning

In the left-hand column below, identify five reasons why a coach may not be able to answer a question. In the right-hand column, identify what you could do to ensure that the questions could be heard and answered.

Unable to answer the question because:	How to ensure questions can be heard and answered:

Now go to Appendix A, page 87

5.3.6 Decision Making and Sharing

Having analysed the evidence presented to you by the candidates through your observation of their performance and subsequent questioning, you should have identified which performance criteria they have and have not achieved or demonstrated competence in. You should now be in a position to share your decisions with them.

You may need a few minutes after the questioning or the review and feedback stage in which to gather your thoughts, complete as much of the paperwork as appropriate and prepare yourself. Do not forget to ensure that the candidate knows why you may need a few minutes.

When you undertake an assessment, either as a practice or for real, you may find that the decisions are made and shared during the earlier review and feedback phase. This is perfectly acceptable practice, but you need to make sure that you fully understand the importance of sharing decisions at the right time, in the right place in the right way.

For those candidates who have performed well, this is often the easiest and most pleasurable phase of the assessment, sharing with them the news that they are competent and able to progress. For those who have not performed well or are not competent across a number of areas, this phase could prove to be a little more challenging.

Have a look at the scenarios below and consider how you would share the decisions with the candidates in each scenario. Remember that, with each candidate, you will need to build an action plan to identify how he or she can progress in the future.

Scenario I

Michael is a very confident and capable coach. Technically, he has a detailed understanding of his sport. He has been coaching for over 20 years, although does not possess any formal coaching qualifications and has hinted on a number of occasions that he sees no use for them.

You have observed that he is a competent coach across all areas except one. During the assessment, you have observed that he has picked up a number of inappropriate or poor habits when addressing the participants. He has only one preferred style of delivery, having adopted a very *telling* approach. He tends to *bark* orders at his participants, particularly the younger ones and at one stage reduced 13-year-old Ben to tears. Michael's response to your questions was that he saw nothing wrong with this style and had been very effective over the years and that *if it ain't broke, he ain't going to fix it.*

This style of coaching is not consistent with the national governing body's preferred delivery styles and conflicts with aspects of their Child Protection code. As such, you have identified that, whilst competent across a number of areas, Michael is not competent here and, as such, you cannot recommend that he pass the qualification.

Scenario 2

Jennifer is a relatively new coach in her sport. Having retired from competition as a result of injury, she has decided she wants to put something back into the sport she loves. She has no formal qualifications but has over 12 years of experience as a national athlete.

You have observed that her technical understanding and ability is first class, but have reservations about her *how to coach* skills. Upon further questioning, she has acknowledged that this might be a weakness but is working hard in her coaching practice with her old coach and now mentor to understand how to teach or coach participants to improve. Whilst this is an ongoing concern in terms of Jennfier's professional development and growth as a coach, you have noted that she is committed to learn and improve her coaching style and delivery methods. You have identified that she presents no threat to the participants' safety, have found her to be competent and can recommend to the national governing body that she pass the qualification.

It is important to ensure that the candidate is aware of exactly which areas they are and are not competent in. As with the middle stage of the praise burger, you may well be expected to identify how, when and where candidates did not achieve the assessment criteria or evidence competence. Candidates may well expect you to evidence exactly when, where and how they did not achieve the criteria and you should be capable of doing this. Your notes, the completed assessment criteria and national governing body guidelines may well help you to provide that evidence.

5.3.7 Feedback and Action Planning

At this point, you will have recorded whether or not the person being assessed has achieved any of the performance/assessment criteria and you will have recorded your observations, questions asked and responses received.

Once the formal observation and questioning has been completed, a review and feedback sessions needs to be undertaken with the person being assessed. In order to identify the principles of an effective review, work through the following activity:

ACTIVITY 19 – Conducting a review

Read the four statements from fictitious assessors offered at the end of an assessment. Briefly comment on each. In the last row of the table try to identify the sequence of events in a good review session.

Assessor 1
'Well, you've failed, as I knew you would. I suppose I'll see you again, although I'm not sure you're cut out for this. You haven't met any of the performance criteria.'
Comment:
Assessor 2
'I've enjoyed what I've seen. You seemed to be quite involved in the session. Some of the points you made were good, some of the organisation was OK, you looked smart and you did quite well. However, I'm really not sure if I can pass you because there were some things you did not do very well. On balance, I don't think I can actually pass you today. What do you think?'
Comment:
Assessor 3
'I'm sorry I've got to rush off. I'll give you a ring in a day or two when I've time to let you know how you've done.'
Comment:
Assessor 4
'Thank you for the session. I'd like to ask one or two questions. How did you feel you did?. Yes, I pretty much agree with you. How do you think you could have improved on that, then?. I thought your preparation and performance were excellent, except that one area you also identified for improvement. I'd like to suggest you go and work on this, then come back to me when you feel ready.
Comment:
Sequence of events in a good feedback session

 Now go to Appendix A, page 88

In gathering evidence to justify your competence as an assessor, you will be required to show you have undertaken an effective review and provided constructive with the candidate. You will also be required to show how you provided a written record for the person being assesses to take away.

How to Conduct an Effective Review and Feedback Session

A review is often made up of three key stages:

1 Firstly, a **debrief** is conducted with the candidate to identify, among other things, what went well during the assessment.

2 In the second stage, **areas for improvement** are often identified.

3 Finally, a **summary** is given focusing on the positive aspects of the session.

A review and feedback session is often best conducted as a *praise burger*. This involves providing an overview of the candidate's strengths first, then identifying areas for their improvement as an assessor and, finally, reinforcing their strengths and good practice in a summary.

You may find that this phase of the assessment process merges with the latter phases of decision-making and sharing as well as action planning. This is perfectly acceptable practice.

While you are learning about your role as an assessor, it is important to understand and conduct each distinct phase, even if they are merged into one larger less discrete phase after the observation and questioning.

Debrief

Having completed the assessment using observation and questioning as tools to gather and analyse the candidate's evidence, you should be in a position to identify some of the candidate's key strengths. In the first instance, you may encourage the candidate to identify what they feel their strengths were. You can then expand further on their observations to reinforce good practice. In addition, you may identify other areas of strengths or good practice that were evidenced during the assessment but not identified as such by the candidate.

How would you open the debrief session? Having completed Activity 19, is there anything you can learn about what to do and what not to do as an assessor during this phase of the process?

A good debrief will also give you plenty of information about your own performance as an assessor. You could, for instance, find out about:

- anything you omitted to do or say that should have been in the briefing but was not
- the quality of information you gave to the person being assessed
- the quality and clarity of the questions you asked
- anything the person being assessed did that you failed to see or interpreted wrongly
- the quality of a simulation
- whether you were supportive or threatening.

Areas for Improvement

This part of the review can often be the most difficult for assessors; particularly if their candidate has not performed well during the assessment. Your manner, that is they way in which you conduct this stage of the review and feedback is critical to ensure the candidates confidence in the assessment process and their continued commitment.

> Imagine yourself as a coach feeding back to the participant. How many teaching or coaching points do you offer at any one time? Which points do you choose to focus on? What language or words do you use? What body language do you adopt? How do you look to use those teaching or coaching points to help the participant develop their skills and performance.

Part of your role is not only to determine whether or not the candidate is competent but also to enable their growth and development in their role. Remember that, even if an individual has achieved all of the performance criteria, they will have still areas of weakness to further develop or refine to ensure that they are the very best they can be at their job.

As such, during this stage of the review and feedback you will have to be very clear with your observations and feedback and, more significantly, reinforce these with actual examples of how, when and where the areas for improvement or weaknesses were evidenced. This will provide you with a foundation to build on in identifying how the candidate can move forward or develop in their role.

> You may find that you are already starting to conduct aspects of the action-planning phase here. Make sure that you record all relevant observations and comments about how the candidate has suggested they might be able to address areas of weakness.

During this stage, you should invite and expect questions from the candidate seeking clarification and advice about a number of issues. Complete the following activity to help you anticipate some of the questions you may well have to answer in the future.

ACTIVITY 20 – Seeking clarity and advice

Imagine you are the person being assessed. Write down four questions you might want to ask the assessor.

 Now go to Appendix A, page 90

Summary

Using the praise burger analogy, this is the point at which you should look to revisit and reinforce good practice to ensure the candidate understands when and how they evidenced their strengths or good practice during the session.

It is important that the candidate takes some responsibility or ownership for their performance and the outcome of their session. Self-reflection is an invaluable tool to aid this analysis.

Undertaking a Review and Feedback Checklist	
Do I:	✓ or X
ensure the information I give the person being assessed clearly indicates whether or not the criteria have been met?	
ensure candidates receive a written record?	
give feedback as soon as possible after the session?	
remember that my feedback should encourage confidence and help the person being assessed develop?	
encourage the person being assessed to seek clarification and advice?	
share my notes with the person being assessed?	
use the praise burger effectively (ie praise followed by constructive criticism, followed by praise)?	
use the feedback from the person being assessed to assess your performance as an assessor?	
not just tell, but listen?	

By this phase of the assessment process, you should have evaluated the candidate's performance against the performance criteria and made an assessment of their performance to determine whether they are competent.

Now is the time to look forward and consider the future. Action planning is a critical phase in the development of an individual's competence and growth. This is a goal-setting exercise with the person being assessed, designed to ensure that opportunities for further development are signposted, negotiated and agreed, and recorded.

A good action plan will be determined by the information gained during the assessment (ie through performance/assessment criteria). By the time the review and feedback stage comes, you should have a clear idea about this, as you have seen the candidate's performance. The action plans will be determined by the the outcome of the assessment.

ACTIVITY 21 – Developing an action plan

Write down the action plan for the outcomes achieved below:

Assessment Outcome	Action Plan
Not yet competent	
Competent	

➡ **Now go to Appendix A, page 91**

Your candidate may have had difficulty with some parts of the assessment and so failed to demonstrate competence. They will need your help, support and advice to make up the ground. During the final stages of your review, you must agree a suitable course of action – one that will put things right and encourage future success without demotivating. Try not to dictate what the person being assessed should do. Involve them in the review and gain agreement on these issues. The candidate can then draw up a list of things to do which will form the basis of an action plan (ie actions that will provide the additional training and/or the necessary experience). In this way, the candidate goes away from the feedback with some positive ideas.

ACTIVITY 22 – Developing the candidate's performance

Write down four ways in which you can help candidates in your review.

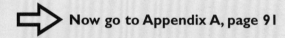 **Now go to Appendix A, page 91**

To help produce an action plan during the feedback, you should:

- identify precisely the criteria achieved or not yet achieved

- give precise reasons why they were achieved or not yet achieved

- explain how they could be achieved in the future.

A key feature of your role is not just to decide whether the candidate is competent, but also to review their learning, guide their progress and aid their development as coaches.

Developing an Action Plan Checklist	
Do I:	✓ or X
negotiate and agree an action plan according to the coach or official's achievements?	
identify remedial help for lower achievements?	
encourage those who demonstrate their competence to look for the next qualification/professional development step?	
encourage those who exceed competence to consider broader experience at the same level or a qualification at a higher level?	

5.3.8 Completing the Documentation

Having completed most of the phases of assessment, you should consider how to manage the documentation and paperwork.

Between the assessor and the person being assessed, there are two kinds of documents that require attention. These are:

- NGB documents
- awarding body forms.

The person responsible for the scheme in your governing body will ensure that the appropriate type of paperwork is always available. Help and advice will be given to you by the centre coordinator or organiser in your national governing body.

Any judgement you make must be supported by:

- an assessment plan
- the evidence of your assessment (observation checklist, copy of questions and answers)
- your assessment outcome record
- a record of feedback and action plans.

You should agree these details with the person being assessed and both of you should clearly sign and date the documents. They can then be used externally with awarding bodies or when you need to present evidence yourself as an assessor.

Any documentation should also be:

- accurate
- readable
- stored securely
- readily available.

These factors all contribute to quality assurance.

5.4 Summary

In this section, you have considered:

- the eight phases of assessment
- the importance of planning an assessment
- what to include and how to conduct a briefing
- how to analyse the evidence using observations and questions as the primary assessment tools
- how to conduct the review and feedback session with the coach
- how to make and share decisions
- how to report the results of your assessment accurately.

5.5 Self-tester 5

You may wish to check you have grasped all the information contained in this final section before undertaking the next sub-section. Try this self-tester without looking back for the answers. This will give you an accurate idea of how much you have understood.

I What are the eight phases of assessment?
•
•
•
•
•
•
•

2 List six things you feel need to be considered in preparing to conduct an assessment in your sport:
•
•
•
•
•
•

3 **Identify the main documents which should be available during the preparation stage:**

-

-

-

4 **Explain why you should or should not use comments from a participant as evidence of achieving a performance criterion:**

5 **Explain how you can ensure the person being assessed is assessed in as natural a way as possible:**

6 **List five main reasons why a person being assessed might fail to answer a question:**

-

-

-

-

-

7 **Describe the action you should take if you think the person being assessed has misunderstood your question:**

8 Explain when you think feedback should be given:

9 Describe the most important things the person being assessed will want to find out from the feedback:

-
-

10 Describe how the person being assessed should feel after you have completed the feedback:

-
-

11 Explain what you could do in the feedback to show the person being assessed that your assessment has been carefully considered and is fair:

12 Write down four things you stand to gain by listening to the comments and questions of the person being assessed:

•	•
•	•

13 Specify who should agree the action plan:

14 Describe a typical action plan for someone who has not achieved all the performance criteria:

15 Describe the sort of action plan you might suggest for someone who proved satisfactory on all criteria:

-
-

16 Describe the four key points regarding paperwork:

•	•
•	•

Check your answers with those in Appendix B. If you had any difficulty, reread this section. If you are still unsure, contact an assessor or verifier within your NGB.

➡ **Now go to Appendix B, page 97**

Section Six

Quality Assurance

6.1 Introduction

Quality assurance is the combination of the systems, people and processes that make your assessments, and those of other assessors, valid and reliable.

Using the driving test scenario, anyone in the vehicle might assume that before leaving the factory, the brakes were checked against a set of standards, were the right ones for the vehicle and were fitted correctly. All such assumptions are part of trusting the worthiness of a product, that it is fit for purpose.

In the same way, people will trust that, as an assessor, you are using the right assessments in the right way with the right candidates.

6.2 Learning Outcomes

By the end of this section, you should be able to:

- explain the importance of quality assurance
- identify the key people involved in quality assurance
- identify ways of contributing to quality assurance.

6.3 Quality Assurers

Successful quality assurance means you can be sure of the quality of a product, process or service. In your case, it is about ensuring the reliability and validity of the assessment decisions you make.

Section Four

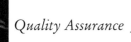
Someone may check your decisions. **Moderators** may re-examine some of the evidence to see if they reach the same conclusions. Moderators check your decisions against the standards used for the coaches you assess.

Verifiers may observe you assessing. This allows them to check you are using the appropriate standards for those you are assessing and, at the same time, observe your performance against the standards for assessors. Verifiers are responsible for ensuring quality assurance within the assessment process – this may include the paperwork and the way in which the assessment process is recorded.

Verification can be done internally or externally. Someone from your governing body may observe you in their role as an **internal verifier** and someone from the awarding body may quality assess the quality assurance right across the assessment spectrum (**external verifier**).

ACTIVITY 23 – Quality assurers

Write down who you think might be involved in quality assurance.

 Now go to Appendix A, page 92

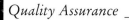

The figure below shows the roles and hierarchy of those individuals involved with quality assuring.

Internal verifiers

Internal verifiers, or verification verifiers, check you are meeting and maintaining the assessor standards, and are looking at the process of assessment and how you carry it out. They will certainly check the paperwork you produce.

External verifiers

External verifiers are a step removed from you. They check the systems and checking processes of the people checking you.

External verifier

Internal verifier

Senior assessor

Senior assessors

Senior assessors, or support verifiers, will probably need to countersign all your assessments while you are still gathering evidence to become fully accredited as an assessor. They are therefore putting their name to any licence to practice, and are quality assuring your assessment of the standards you are assessing. The better they support you, the better your assessment practice is likely to be.

Peer assessors

You may be using other assessors as expert witnesses, or using their assessment to accredit candidates for APA/APL. Or you may be fulfilling that role for them. You need to be sure of their status and they of yours. You also need to ensure there is consistency in assessment practice if more than one of you is assessing the same candidate for different parts of a qualification.

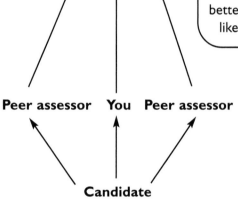

Peer assessor   You   Peer assessor

Candidate

Candidates

Candidates will need to countersign the assessment plan, to show they agree with the planned assessments, the assessment checklists, the record of questions, the outcome, feedback and action planning sheets and any summary sheet used. This demonstrates that they have been involved with the whole process, and that they believe they have been fairly assessed.

Figure 2: The assessment hierarchy

6.4 How to Assure Quality

There are various things you can do to contribute to the quality assurance processes in place.

- **Planning and preparation**
  The better the planning of and preparation for an assessment, the higher the quality is likely to be.

- **Involving the candidate**
  If the assessment process involves the person being assessed as much as possible, then their contribution to the evidence produced will be that much greater.

- **Meeting standards and processes**
  As part of your progress towards accreditation as an assessor, you will need to collect evidence that shows you can meet the standards of assessment as outlined in section five, and that shows you understand and can follow the processes and procedures laid down by your governing or awarding body.

- **Maintaining standards**
  Once you have become accredited as an assessor, you will need to demonstrate that you are continuing to maintain the standards you have previously demonstrated. You may be observed again by a senior assessor, or internal verifier, as part of this ongoing process. Always strive to carry out best practice in your assessing.

- **Recording evidence**
  You can contribute to quality assurance by making sure all the assessment tools are correctly used and completed, in a legible fashion, which is easy for others up the quality assurance ladder to check.

- **Countersigning**
  While you are still collecting evidence to demonstrate your own competence as an assessor, you will need to get all your assessments countersigned by a fully accredited assessor. Your governing body will be able to tell you who can do this.

- **Standardisation meetings**
  You should attend assessor meetings and read any correspondence advising on assessment practice, to ensure your assessments are reliable when compared to other assessors. This also gives you an opportunity to contribute ideas and suggestions to the process.

- **Recommending changes/improvements**
  You can contribute to quality assurance by passing on suggestions for improvements. It is best to make a permanent record of any suggestions you make – they can be used as part of your evidence for accreditation and as evidence of maintaining standards.

- **Continuous professional development (CPD) – keeping up to date**
  As an assessor, you have a duty to keep yourself up to date. Remember, this will apply to at least two sets of standards – the standards used on the person you assess and the assessor standards. Continuing professional development (CPD) is key to this updating process.

6.5   Summary

In this section, you have discovered that quality assurance puts the trust into the system. Everyone has a role to play, but there are specific things you can do to assist.

6.6 Self-tester 6

1   **Why is quality assurance important?**

2   **List three people who can contribute to quality assurance:**

•

•

•

3   **List three things you can do as an assessor to assure quality of assessment:**

•

•

•

Check your answers with those given at the back of the resource. If you had any difficulty, reread this section. If you are still unsure, contact an assessor or verifier within your NGB.

 Now go to Appendix B, page 100

Section Seven

Where Next?

7.1 Introduction

To become an assessor, you will have to be assessed against the standards especially written for your role. The same system you use to assess candidates will apply to you as assessor.

7.2 Learning Outcomes

By the end of this section, you should be able to identify:

- the importance of building up a portfolio of evidence
- key questions to ask your governing or awarding body
- key questions to ask at any assessor training event you may attend
- further resources and contacts you will find useful.

7.3 Portfolio of Evidence

You may have already been acting as an assessor for your governing body. If so, this evidence will form the first part of your portfolio.

 The more evidence a candidate presents, the easier it is to make an assessment decision, provided that it is valid and reliable. The same applies to you as an assessor, so you should:

- keep a logbook including an information section, dates, names and locations
- keep accurate and legible records of everything you do
- analyse your own performance and gain feedback from the people you are assessing
- refer to the criteria laid down for assessors and see if you can start to build up the evidence in your portfolio
- ask someone in a senior position in your governing body to countersign your logbook
- do not forget accreditation of prior learning and experience and record this.

7.4 Further Training

sports coach UK (scUK) offers a variety of workshops and resources related to assessing in sport. See Sections 7.6 and 7.7 for more details.

Sections 7.6 and 7.7

If you are going to attend a workshop organised by your governing body to orientate and accredit assessors, you will be given additional advice on how to assess and how to become accredited as an assessor.

If you are not going to attend a workshop, you will gain support and advice from your national governing body on the standards, registration, assessment and accreditation as an assessor. You will need to apply through an approved centre in order to become accredited.

7.5 Summary

 You will need to ask your national governing body questions to identify the specifics of what you need to do to become fully accredited as an assessor for your sport.

Before attending, check you can:

- describe your role and responsibilities as an assessor
- evaluate a range of assessment tools and select the most appropriate ones for specific assessment situations
- explain the terms *valid* and *reliable* in the context of assessment
- explain the principles of assessing previous learning and achievement
- explain the process of assessment and verification
- outline the eight phases in the assessment process and how it can be applied to your sport.

7.6 Useful Contacts

sports coach UK

sports coach UK (scUK) works closely with sports governing bodies and other partners to provide a comprehensive service for coaches throughout the UK. This includes an extensive programme of workshops, which have proved valuable to coaches from all types of sports and every level of experience. For further details of **scUK** workshops in your area, contact the **scUK** Business Support Centre (BSC). For more details about other membership services such as insurance, contact **scUK**.

sports coach UK Business Support Centre
Sporst Development Centre
Loughborough University
Loughborough
Leicestershire LE11 3TU
Tel: 01509-226130
Fax: 01509-226134
Email: bsc@sportscoachuk.org

sports coach UK
114 Cardigan Road
Headingley
Leeds LS6 3BJ
Tel: 0113-274 4802
Fax: 0113-275 5019
Email: coaching@sportscoachuk.org
Website: www.sportscoachuk.org

NGBs

The national governing body for your sport or activity will give advice on assessor courses and other relevant information. National governing body contact details are available from:

Central Council of Physical Recreation (CCPR)
Francis House
Francis Street
London SW1P 1DE
Tel: 020-7854 8500
Fax: 020-7854 8501
Email: info@ccpr.org.uk
Website: www.ccpr.org.uk

1st4sport Qualifications

1st4sport Qualifications is the awarding body for the Introduction to Assessment Practice in Sport (IAPS) qualification. They will be able to signpost you to approved centres delivering this qualification.

1st4sport Qualifications
Coachwise Ltd
Chelsea Close
Off Amberley Road
Armley
Leeds LS12 4HP
Fax: 0113-231 9606
Email: enquiries@1st4sportqualifications.com
Website: www.1st4sportqualifications.com

ENTO

The Employment National Training Organisation (ENTO) is the guardian of the assessor and verifier standards (A1, A2, V1 and V2). They will be able to signpost you to further information about there standards and to approved centres delivering them.

The Employment National Training Organisation (ENTO)
4th Floor
Kimberley House
47 Vaughan Way
Leicester LE1 4SG
Tel: 0116-251 7979
Fax: 0116-251 1464
Email: info@ento.co.uk
Website: www.ento.co.uk

Appendix A

Feedback: Activities

Section One

ACTIVITY 2 – Qualities and characteristics of an assessor

You will probably have picked out similar points to these:

Assessor 1

- *The person being assessed is not told what is going to happen and has no say in it.*
- *The assessor appears to be very aggressive.*
- *The assessment sounds more like a threat than an opportunity.*
- *The assessor does not appear to care about the candidate's feelings.*

Assessor 2

- *The candidate is not prepared for an important experience.*
- *The assessor tells the person being assessed it is not too serious (calls it nonsense).*
- *The assessor is hinting at some sort of 'fait accompli'.*

Assessor 3

- *Unnecessary jargon is being used which could confuse or even put the person being assessed off the idea of assessment.*
- *The assessor is creating unnecessary barriers.*

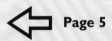 Page 5

Section Two

ACTIVITY 3 – What, how and where

Compare you answers with those offered below:

What you think you will actually do as an assessor.

What: *you judge whether or not the person is able to do the role. The role might be as a coach, an official, a tutor or an assessor. In the same way that the driving test examiner assesses whether people can start, steer and manoeuvre the car, so an assessor in sport checks whether people can meet all the competences set down in the standards for the role being assessed.*

The main method(s) you will use to conduct the assessment and check competence.

How: *A competence-based qualification means a coach can actually coach or that an official can actually officiate. One of the main ways you can check whether or not someone can meet the role is to watch them, just as a driving test examiner watches people drive. The driving test examiner will ask questions about the Highway Code; you will ask questions to make sure the person being assessed has the knowledge to support his or her skills. Assessment can take place at any time, so candidates can gain a competence-based qualification whenever they are ready.*

Where you think you should conduct the assessment.

Where: *Competence-based qualifications are all about performance in the workplace. The driving test examiner tests the driver on the road, not in a test centre. Similarly, assessors in sport must assess candidates at the poolside, at the track, on the court, on the field or in the gym.*

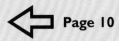 **Page 10**

Section Three

ACTIVITY 4 – Observation

Jot down some of the points you might be able to observe when watching a coach in your sport. An example is given to help you.

Include two or three factors which you need to consider to ensure the assessment is valid and reliable.

- *Know the standards against which I am assessing inside out*

- *Organisation of environment and group*

- *Safety factors/issues*

- *Coach/performer relationship, official/performer relationship, tutor/learner relationship, or assessor/candidate relationship*

- *Session structure and progression*

- *Demonstration of skills*

- *Use of feedback*

- *Knowledge and application of techniques, tactics and rules of the sport.*

Identify any difficulties or limitations in direct observation.

- *It may only provide a one-off snapshot of the person's competence.*

- *It is dependent upon the objectivity of the assessor.*

- *It is expensive in terms of time and human resources.*

- *Some aspects may be difficult to observe.*

- *It does not check knowledge or understanding.*

- *It is not always possible to observe someone in a realistic environment, using natural evidence (ie evidence that normally happens as part of a session or a competition).*

- *It is not easy to observe changes over time.*

 Page 16

ACTIVITY 5 – Recording observations

You may have considered the following strengths and weaknesses, and possible solutions to overcome any disadvantages:

Method	Advantage	Disadvantage	Possible Solution
National Governing Body Checklist	*Standardised* *Both candidate and assessor know the criteria and paperwork to be used*	*You need to know the paperwork well to navigate it easily while still observing the candidate*	*Familiarisation of paperwork before assessment*
Personal Notes	*You can write as you see things happen*	*Needs extra time to transfer these notes onto the NGB documentation*	*Familiarisation of paperwork before assessment* *Plan sufficient time for transfer*
Audio Tape	*Can be used in the rain* *Can be an accurate record of what was said*	*Needs to be transferred onto paperwork* *Can be disconcerting to the candidate*	*Plan sufficient time to transfer* *Keep sufficient distance from candidate and keep voice low* *Allow time for candidate to become at ease with being recorded*
Video Tape	*Allows observation of changes over time* *Useful for post-assessment standardisation or comparison sessions with other assessors*	*Needs special equipment and familiarity with that equipment* *Not always easy to be in the right position and remain unobtrusive*	*Familiarisation with equipment before assessment* *Plan positioning before assessment*

In most cases, the solutions link to pre-planning of the assessment, which will be covered further in a later section.

Page 17

ACTIVITY 6 – Other assessment methods

You may have listed some of the more traditional methods, such as:

Assessment Method	Strengths	Weaknesses
Assignments and projects	Requires coaches to apply sports knowledge	Favours those who write well
Case studies	Useful for assessing long-term strategies	Marking can be subjective
Multiple-choice and short answer questions	Objective and easily marked	Test of memory; not application
Open-booktests	Allows candidates to learn while being assessed	Takes time to mark
Examinations	Tests knowledge and understanding	Stressful for candidates
Oral questioning	Checks understanding	Time-consuming

 Page 18

ACTIVITY 7 – Using APA/APL

You might have suggested:

- current NGB coach awards
- things the candidate has written (eg plans, reports, articles, written documents)
- records of what the coach or official has done (eg diaries, logbooks)
- letters of validation/ testimony (eg from colleagues, employers, participants)
- academic achievements, certificates and awards.

Remember the portfolio of evidence can be derived from any valid source or combination of sources but must fulfil the criteria of validity, currency, authenticity and sufficiency. Questioning is also likely to provide additional information or assist with ensuring authenticity or currency. If you are in any doubt, you should seek help from your internal verifier (probably a regional or national coach or official of your governing body).

 Page 23

Compare your table with the one below:

Performance Criteria	Methods of Assessment	Sample Questions
Participants are physically and mentally prepared to participate	*Observation checklist* *Questioning* *Assignment* *Case study*	*In what other ways could you make sure participants are prepared physically and mentally?*
All communications are clear, accurate and presented in a style appropriate to the participants	*Observation checklist* *Questioning* *Case study*	*How would you communicate with a different group (eg the elderly)?*
Explanations/demonstrations are clear, technically correct and appropriate to the participants	*Observation checklist* *Questioning* *Multiple-choice questions* *Assignment*	*What other methods of demonstration could you use and when would you use them?*
Participants are encouraged and motivated throughout the session	*Observation checklist* *Questioning*	*How might you deal with participants who are disappointed by their performance?*
Prior experiences are correctly identified	*Questioning* *Case study* *Assignment*	*What methods can you use to identify prior experiences?*
Feedback aims to raise the participants' self-esteem and motivation	*Observation checklist* *Questioning*	*What other methods of feedback can you use?*

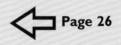 **Page 26**

Section Four

ACTIVITY 9 – Fair selection

You have been asked to select a team, crew or squad for a match.

How would you ensure the selection is fair?

By having clear criteria laid out and agreed beforehand, it's easier to select the team fairly and justify that selection.

What could happen if no criteria are used?

Without any criteria for selecting a team, it is possible to be accused of bias, favouritism, unfair practice or inequitable behaviour.

 **Page 32**

ACTIVITY 10 – Reliable assessment

There are a number of things that could affect the reliability of your assessment. You have to make sure you:

- are clear about what you are assessing (ie the criteria are written down)

- know the job (this is why it is essential that assessors are coaches or officials in that sport)

- are not biased by factors such as age, sex, looks, clothes

- do not let personal factors interfere with your assessment (eg an instinctive like or dislike for someone).

 **Page 33**

Section Five

ACTIVITY 11 – Planning for the assessment

Compare your schedule with the sample one below:

General	
Sport: *Basketball*	Date: *26 January*
Time: *10.00am to 11.30am*	Venue: *Sports hall*

Level of Award	
Number of participants: *10–12*	Experience of participants: *Juniors*
Age of participants: *13–15*	

The person being assessed has planned to do the following:

a session taking one and a half hours in which participants will be introduced to a new technique as part of their 10-session course (this is the third session).

Environment/Facility Requirements	Equipment Required
One free from distraction that has been checked against the governing body safety code.	What equipment does the candidate plan to use? • *12 basketballs* • *cones* • *bibs*
	What equipment and paperwork do you, the assessor, need? *NGB checklists, tape recorder and blank tapes, blank paper and pens/pencils.*

Significant Others	
Who else might be affected by the session? *Sports centre manager/receptionist to ensure session is booked and equipment is available and that the sports hall is set up for the session staff.* *The internal verifier may be required.*	Who is going to make contact with them? *It is the candidate's responsibility to organise the session, the facilities, and the equipment.* *The assessor will inform the internal verifier.*

Briefing

What should the person being assessed produce for you to see (assess) before the session begins? *Session plan and logbook/ portfolio.*	What are you going to need to discuss with the candidate and how should it be recorded? *Review the plan and discuss. Make any amendments as necessary. Produce an assessment plan with the candidate. Discuss and agree assessment criteria. Discuss and agree the form of the assessment.*

Session Observation Checklist

Produce a simple checklist which ensures you remember to record evidence against the agreed performance criteria and ranges:

- *Previous experience*
- *Presentation/demonstration*
- *Participant understanding*
- *Warm-up*
- *Any demonstration is technically correct*

- *Analysis of participant performance*
- *Correction*
- *Cool-down*
- *Future work.*

Standard Oral Questions Prepared

What questions might you ask to cover the six performance criteria?

- *What other methods of warm-up could you use?*
- *What other methods of presenting skills and techniques could you use?*

- *What would you have done differently if the participants were elderly/teenagers/ de-motivated?*
- *Plus additional questions arising from the candidate's performance.*

Portfolio of Supplementary Evidence

What other evidence might you find in logbooks/portfolios to infer competence against the criteria?	*Review logbooks, plus any additional evidence provided by the candidate, session plans of other lessons, feedback from participants, testimonies from employers, assessments by other assessors, records of communications.*

Feedback to Candidate	
What three things should you include within your feedback? • *What the person did well* • *Where the person did not do well* • *Guidance on what to do next* • *A clear outcome.*	How will you record this feedback? *On the appropriate NGB documentation.*
Paperwork	
What paperwork will the person being assessed require? *Assessment plan, observation checklist, record of questions and answers, outcome, feedback and action plan report.*	What paperwork should you, the assessor, keep? *Assessment plan, and outcome and action plan report. When gathering evidence for the vocational assessor standards, assessors should keep copies of all documents generated.*

← Page 41

ACTIVITY 12 – Additional requirements

Some coaches may need special or additional preparation.

Type of Coach	Additional Requirements
You may have considered that the person being assessed might be disabled in some way. For example, the person may have: • *a hearing or sight impairment* • *a physical disability* • *a temporary disability after sporting injury* • *some form of learning difficulty* • *dyslexia.*	*If it does not affect their activity, it does not matter. You must ensure that candidates with special needs have the help and support they require. You may need to consider:* • *the type of instructions and questions you give* • *whether the person being assessed needs additional support or equipment* • *the assessment tools you use and possible adaptations.*

← Page 44

ACTIVITY 13 – Knowing yourself

Check your answers with the interpretation below:

Type of Person	Meaning
The *halo effect* candidate	*The halo effect candidate comes with a reputation already – has been doing it for years in their own way and is bound to get the qualification.*
The *horns effect* candidate	*The horns effect candidate – just rubs some people up and evokes a negative reaction in some people. Will be lucky to get anywhere near a qualification.*
The *cuddly bunny effect* candidate	*The cuddly bunny effect candidate – really nice person. Would be upset not to get the qualification. Deserves the qualification just for turning up.*
The *perfectionist effect* assessor	*The perfectionist effect assessor – 'Nobody passes unless they really impress me. They have to be at least up to my standard'. Only people above the level of the qualification will get it.*
The *ruthless executive effect* assessor	*The ruthless executive effect assessor – 'Too much sloppiness around here'. Changes need to be made to give a few people a shock. One or two candidates will not get their qualification just to teach everyone else a lesson.*
The *hate-to-offend effect* assessor	*The hate-to-offend effect assessor – hates to upset anyone. Cannot bear the thought of having a failure. All the candidates get their qualification to avoid causing problems or conflict in the future.*
The *play-it-safe effect* assessor	*The play-it-safe effect assessor – always gives the benefit of the doubt. Thinks that everyone should be given a chance, regardless of what they are like. Has made dithering into an art form. Another one who will give out qualifications.*

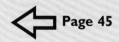

Page 45

ACTIVITY 14 – Preparing facilities

In preparing the facilities, your answers should have addressed some of the following:

Facilities	Responsibility
• Somewhere to plan the assessment and brief the candidate • Access permissions and arrangements to access all areas to be used • Access considerations for people of differing needs • The area to be used in the session • Equipment to be used for the session • Clothing to be worn • An examination room • Somewhere to debrief the candidate • Knowing the weather forecast • Alternatives in case of bad weather.	

Page 46

ACTIVITY 15 – Impact on others

You may have given some of the following answers:

Others
• The person being assessed • The 'guinea pigs' being used for the session • Parents • Key holders • Other users of the facility, area or equipment • Other activities going on at the same time • Internal verifiers or senior assessors • Facility managers • Bookings personnel.

Page 47

ACTIVITY 16 – Briefing candidates

You might have given some of the following answers:

- *Do you understand exactly what is expected?*
- *Do you still feel ready for the assessment?*
- *Is there anything you wish to change?*
- *Do you understand how to achieve the performance criteria according to the national governing body's systems and methods?*
- *Do you have any questions?*

⇐ **Page 48**

ACTIVITY 17 – Golden rules of observation

You might have given some of the following answers:

- *Make sure you can see and hear what is going on*
- *Be an unobtrusive observer*
- *Only use specified and agreed criteria to assess*
- *Only assess what the person being assessed actually does*
- *Only assess what you actually see (comments from participants are not always helpful)*
- *If you are not sure what a criterion means, or whether the person being assessed has achieved it, ask*
- *Make sure simulations are as close as possible to the real thing*
- *Do not help/lead or hinder the person being assessed.*

⇐ **Page 49**

ACTIVITY 18 – Effective questioning

You may have given some of the following answers:

Unable to answer the question because:	How to ensure questions can be heard and answered because:
The person being assessed may not know the answer	*You cannot do anything about this*
The person being assessed may not have heard clearly	*The person being assessed may not have heard clearly, so ask again, more clearly*

The question is inappropriate, wrong or outside the essential knowledge area.	*The question is wrong, so make sure the question tests the agreed areas.*
The question is right but has not been asked clearly.	*The question was not asked clearly, so ask the person being assessed if the question is unclear. Tell the person being assessed not to guess, but to seek clarification first and then answer the question. If there is a problem, restate the question.*
The person being assessed is in some way disadvantaged.	*You may need to get help on how to deal with this from a colleague or your internal verifier.*
The candidate's mind is not on the task in hand because of some problem (maybe personal).	*There is some other problem, so give the person being assessed the opportunity to talk. Refer the person being assessed to a friend or appropriate authority. Reschedule the assessment if necessary.*

⬅ **Page 50**

ACTIVITY 19 – Conducting a review

Compare your comments with those offered here. How similar is your review and feedback sequence?

Assessor 1

'Well, you've failed, as I knew you would. I suppose I'll see you again, although I'm not sure you're cut out for this. You haven't met any of the performance criteria.'

Comment:

- *Did not ask any relevant questions.*
- *Was not positive or constructive or offer any advice to develop a personal action plan.*

Assessor 2

'I've enjoyed what I've seen. You seemed to be quite involved in the session. Some of the points you made were good, some of the organisation was OK, you looked smart and you did quite well. However, I'm really not sure if I can pass you because there were some things you did not do very well. On balance, I don't think I can actually pass you today. What do you think?'

Comment:

- *Did not inform the person being assessed clearly whether or not the performance criteria have been met.*
- *Did not ask any questions to allow the candidate to demonstrate their competence in a wider context.*
- *Did not give clear explanations for the outcome of the assessment.*

Assessor 3

'I'm sorry I've got to rush off. I'll give you a ring in a day or two when I've time to let you know how you've done.'

Comment:

- *Did not plan in time for the debrief.*
- *Did not give enough time to provide immediate feedback.*

Assessor 4

'Thank you for the session. I'd like to ask one or two questions. How did you feel you did? ... Yes, I pretty much agree with you. How do you think you could have improved on that, then? ...Yes, good point. Here are the notes I made on the session. I thought your preparation and performance were excellent, except that one area you also identified for improvement. I'd like to suggest you go and work on this, then come back to me when you feel ready. How would that be? ... How would you work on this?'

Comment:

- *Did not encourage the coach or official to ask for clarification and advice.*

Sequence of Events in a Good Feedback Session

- *Plan in and allow time for the debrief.*
- *Be positive, for your job is to help candidates and encourage them to continue to develop their skills and seek higher levels of competence.*
- *Encourage the coach or official to ask for clarification and advice. Remember, an interview always involves at least two parties, and as the old saying goes 'you have two ears and only one mouth', so listen twice as much as you speak.*
- *Ask relevant questions. By inserting one or two pertinent questions, it may not be necessary to arrange a further assessment, because the person being assessed may be able to justify the performance. Maybe the person being assessed knew something about the participants that you did not.*
- *Involve the candidates in their own assessment. If you ask candidates to assess their own performance, they become owners of their own development. They are also likely to tell you what they think went well and what did not go well.*

- *Give feedback as soon as possible after performance.*

- *Give clear explanations for the result.*

- *Inform the person being assessed clearly whether or not the performance criteria have been met. Explain which performance criteria have been passed and give praise for these. Explain which have not been met and offer advice on how to proceed. Remember that criticism is more readily accepted if praise has first been given for the parts that were good.*

- *Offer clear advice about what to do next. Try to end on a positive note whatever the outcome. This way the person being assessed is much more likely to tackle the weaknesses and return for the next assessment in a positive way.*

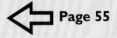
Page 52

ACTIVITY 20 – Seeking clarity and advice

See if your questions match the following suggestions. You will probably find some are the same and some are different:

- *What did I do to make you think my performance was excellent on that element?*

- *What exactly did I do wrong (or fail to do) on that element?*

- *How should I handle that awkward simulation next time?*

- *It was useful talking to parents. Should I do this more often?*

- *How can I develop my interpersonal skills?*

- *OK, I'm not too good at that so, what can I do to get it right next time?*

- *What other things do I need to cover to complete the qualification?*

- *How can I progress to the next level?*

Page 55

Content:

ACTIVITY 21 – Developing an action plan

Check your answers against those below:

Assessment Outcome	Action Plan
Not yet competent	• Identify what experience the person being assessed needs to gain – and how. • Identify what training the person being assessed needs to attend. • Identify what support the person being assessed needs to access – and how. • Arrange further assessment opportunities.
Competent	• Develop breadth of experience. • Apply skills in new contexts/ environments. • Advance to the next level. • Guidelines about how to achieve this.

 Page 58

ACTIVITY 22 – Developing the candidate's performance

Read the following suggestions:

- *A candidate who performed well will probably wish to know the next step in training and qualification.*
- *A candidate who performed less well should be encouraged through proper advice to concentrate on improving poorer areas of performance.*
- *Ensure the person being assessed is properly prepared if a simulation has to be repeated.*
- *Encourage candidates to recognise their achievements even if they have not done a full qualification.*
- *Help candidates recognise they could be ready for additional responsibility (eg to become involved in regional coaching or officiating).*
- *Encourage candidates to feel they are part of a system which is working for and not against them.*

 Page 59

Section Six

ACTIVITY 23 – Quality assurers

You might have given some of the following answers:

- **Candidates** – they want to be sure they have been assessed fairly.
- **Peer assessors** – these are other assessors working with you or on the same site. Your actions can reflect on their abilities and reputations.
- **Senior assessors** – they may be responsible for you as an assessor.
- **Internal verifiers** – their job is to check the processes have been followed correctly.
- **External verifiers** – they check the people who check you.

And don't forget yourself – you are a defender and promoter of at least two sets of standards: the ones you are assessing the candidate against and the standards for assessors.

 **Page 66**

Appendix B

Check Your Understanding: Self-testers

Self-tester 1

1 Consider and outline the role you plan to take on and the standards you think you will need to be aware of:	
My role:	Assessor Senior assessor Verifier Senior tutor Senior referee
I will be working against the following standards:	Assessor standards
I will be assessing the following types of people:	Coaches Officials Assessors Tutors Ground staff
I will be assessing against the following standards:	National Occupational Standards Coaching standards Rules of the game Tutoring standards Assessing standards Health and safety standards Codes of ethics
The awarding body is:	National governing body Awarding body
I will be gaining the following assessor qualification:	A1 CIASL A2 IAPS V1 NGB assessor V2 CRA

I will be assessing people for the following qualifications:	NVQ *Coaching qualification*

2   List three types of people who can benefit from good assessment practice. Give one reason why they benefit for each type:

The candidate – kitemark of quality.
The assessor – can be trusted.
Parents or spectator – can trust the scheme and the qualification-holders.
People who come into contact with the qualification holder – benefit from better sport.

3   List six qualities a good assessor will use when assessing:

Open, patient, honest, knowledgeable, fair, serious, sympathetic, helpful, competent, trustworthy, unprejudiced, empathetic.

 Page 7

Self-tester 2

I   Explain the following terms:

- ***Elements*** *are subsections of units and are discrete parts of a unit.*
- ***Ranges*** *are the different scenarios that need to be covered in a qualification.*
- ***Evidence specifications*** *detail how much or how many of the ranges and criteria need to be covered for the qualification.*

2   Describe three ways in which you can establish your governing body's standards for the performance criteria:

- *Check any governing body rules, codes and guidelines.*
- *Discuss how performance criteria are handled with other assessors.*
- *Cross-check your findings with your internal verifier.*

3   Explain how the assessment system makes sure every candidate is assessed by the same standards:

- *The same performance criteria are used for everyone, by using standardised assessment tools and assessment processes, involving the candidate.*

 **Page 13**

Self-tester 3

1 Allocate a preferred order to the following methods of assessment for competence-based qualifications (some may have the same number):

Method	First Priority	Second Priority	Third Priority
Assignments			✓
Case Studies			✓
Multiple-choice Questions			✓
Observation	✓		
Projects			✓
Simulation		✓	

2 Write down one advantage and one disadvantage of each type of assessment:

Method	Advantage	Disadvantage
Case Studies	*Requires application* *Longer-term measure*	*Favours literate* *Time consuming*
Multiple-choice Questions	*Objective* *Tests knowledge*	*Guessing* *May not test understanding*
Observation	*Watch person in action* *Tests real people with real clients* *Test person's performances*	*Snapshot* *Time consuming* *Cannot check for understanding*
Questioning	*Checks understanding* *Probes* *Supplements*	*Threatening* *Subjective* *Time consuming*
Simulation	*Watch coach or official in action* *Easier to set up than observation*	*Snapshot* *Unrealistic*

3 Explain what is meant by:

APL: a method of allowing people being assessed who have considerable experience to demonstrate their knowledge and understanding by supplying evidence.

Candidates might provide:

- *written reports and articles*
- *diaries and logbooks*
- *letters of validation from colleagues, employers*
- *academic achievements, certificates, awards.*

Criteria: The criteria should be the same as for any other candidate.

4 Why is it important to record your decisions clearly?

- *Your records will be checked by the governing body or awarding body.*
- *A candidate may wish to use these records for APL/APA in the future.*
- *So that everyone is clear about what has, and has not, been achieved.*

 Page 28

Self-tester 4

I Explain what is meant by reliability in assessment:

An assessment is deemed to have reliability if the same result is obtained when carried out by any other competent assessor or if the same standard of performance always produces the same result.

2 Explain what is meant by validity in assessment:

An assessment is deemed to be valid if it actually assesses the competence of the person being assessed for each criteria.

3 **It is possible that the person being assessed could be disadvantaged or disabled in some way. Jot down some considerations you would make to ensure your assessment is fair:**

Think carefully about any instructions you give and make sure they are clear. Check whether the candidate needs additional support or equipment.

4 **Explain how you can ensure the person being assessed can really achieve the performance criteria (it is not just a stroke of luck):**

By assessing over a period of time, rather than just the once.

 Page 34

Self-tester 5

1 **What are the eight phases of assessment?**

1 *Planning*
2 *Briefing*
3 *Analysing the evidence*
4 *Reviewing and giving feedback*
5 *Decision-making and sharing*
6 *Action planning*
7 *Documentation.*

2 **List six things you feel need to be considered in preparing to conduct an assessment in your sport:**

You should consider what:
*   *is being assessed*
*   *governing body standards exist*
*   *makes up an assessment*
*   *paperwork needs preparing*
*   *you know of the coach or official*
*   *you know of yourself*
*   *facilities need preparing*
*   *impact the assessment could have on other people.*

3 Identify the main documents which should be available during the preparation stage:

- *The standards being assessed against*
- *Your NGB documentation*
- *Awarding body documentation.*

4 Explain why you should or should not use comments from a participant as evidence of achieving a performance criterion:

Comments should be used as evidence only after very careful consideration. You should firstly assess what you see the person being assessed do. The comments from a participant may help to clarify or add to your observations. Sometimes a participant may try to influence your judgement.

5 Explain how you can ensure the person being assessed is assessed in as natural a way as possible:

The assessment is done in the working environment of the person being assessed or a near simulation and the assessor must be as unobtrusive as possible (ie stay out of the way and do not help or hinder).

6 List five main reasons why a person being assessed might fail to answer a question:

Your answers may have included the following:
- *The person being assessed may not know the answer.*
- *The person being assessed may not have heard clearly.*
- *The question is inappropriate, wrong or outside the essential knowledge area.*
- *The question is right but has not been asked clearly.*
- *The person being assessed is in some way disadvantaged.*
- *The candidate's mind is not on the task in hand because of some problem (maybe personal).*

7 Describe the action you should take if you think the person being assessed has misunderstood your question:

Restate it and then check the person being assessed understands it.

8 Explain when you think feedback should be given:

The best time for feedback is as soon as possible after the assessment so that you put the person being assessed at ease, and while the assessment is still fresh in their mind.

9 Describe the most important things the person being assessed will want to find out from the feedback:

- *What was achieved and why.*
- *What was not achieved and why.*

10 Describe how the person being assessed should feel after you have completed the feedback:

If you got the right mixture and correct order of praise and criticism, the person being assessed should:

- *feel encouraged and confident*
- *be motivated to develop through training and qualifications*
- *be motivated to correct things that went wrong.*

11 Explain what you could do in the feedback to show the person being assessed that your assessment has been carefully considered and is fair:

Show the person being assessed any notes you kept and comments you made, and gain their agreement of them as a fair and accurate record.

12 Write down four things you stand to gain by listening to the comments and questions of the person being assessed:

Any of the following:
- *Knowledge of your own performance as an assessor (eg were you supportive or threatening).*
- *Things you omitted to do, or things you said you would do in the feedback but did not.*
- *The quality of information you gave to the person being assessed.*
- *The quality and clarity of the questions you asked.*
- *Things the person being assessed did that you failed to see or misinterpreted.*
- *The quality of your simulation.*

13 Specify who should agree the action plan:

The person being assessed and the assessor.

14 Describe a typical action plan for someone who has not achieved all the performance criteria:

- *Identify what experience the person being assessed needs to gain – and how.*
- *Identify what training the person being assessed needs to attend.*
- *Identify what support the person being assessed needs to access – and how.*
- *Arrange further assessment opportunities.*

15 Describe the sort of action plan you might suggest for someone who proved satisfactory on all criteria:

- *Develop breadth of experience*
- *Apply skills in new contexts/environments*
- *Advance to the next level*
- *Guidelines about how to achieve this.*

16 Describe the four key points regarding paperwork:

Paperwork should be:
- accurate
- readable
- stored securely
- readily available.

 Page 61

Self-tester 6

1 Why is quality assurance important?

- *Quality assurance is the combination of the systems, people and processes which make assessments trustworthy and reliable.*
- *People will trust that you as an assessor are using the right assessments in the right way with the right candidates.*

2 List three people who can contribute to quality assurance:

- *Candidates*
- *Peer assessors*
- *Senior assessors*
- *Internal verifiers*
- *External verifiers*
- *You! You are a defender and promoter of at least two sets of standards – the ones you are assessing the candidate against and the standards for assessors.*

3 List three things you can do as an assessor to assure quality of assessment:

- *Planning and preparation*
- *Involve the candidate*
- *Meeting standards and processes*
- *Maintaining standards*
- *Recording evidence*
- *Countersigning*
- *Standardisation meetings*
- *CPD – keeping up to date*
- *Recommending changes/improvements.*

 Page 69

Appendix C

Glossary of Terms

Glossary of Terms	
A1	Assessor qualification, *Assess Candidates Using a Range of Methods.*
A2	Assessor qualification, *Assess Candidates Using Observation.*
Accreditation of Prior Achievement (APA)	Achievement or qualification undergone by an individual in the past, considered towards a different qualification.
Accreditation of Prior Learning (APL)	Learning or experience undergone by an individual in the past and not previously assessed.
Accredited Assessor	An assessor approved by a governing body or awarding body to act as an assessor in a specified context.
Assessment	The process of collecting evidence and making judgements against a specified set of standards.
Awarding Body	A body which awards qualifications. The QCA or SQA has a qualifications framework to approve awarding bodies, including City & Guilds, 1st4Sport Qualifications, British Amateur Gymnastics Association, OCR.
Candidate	The learner who is seeking accreditation as a coach, tutor, assessor or official.
Coach or Official	Anyone who coaches or officiates, teaches or gives instruction through sport.
Competence	The ability to perform the activities of a job/role to clearly defined standards.
Core Unit	Units of competence that are common to a number of occupations, functions, N/SVQs.
Element (of competence)	Subtask(s) of a major task (unit) which describes what an individual should be able to do.

Employment National Training Organisation (ENTO)	The body responsible for drawing up the standards for assessors.
IAPS	Assessor qualification *Introduction to Assessment Practice in Sport*.
National Governing Body (NGB)	A body responsible for maintaining standards in a particular sport.
National Occupational Standards (NOS)	A set of standards agreed by the Sector Skills Council and the National Training Organisations.
National Training Organisation (NTO)	A body responsible for drawing up the industry standards.
National Vocational Qualifications (NVQs)	A qualification based on industry standards, operating in England, Wales and Northern Ireland.
Performance Criteria	Indicate the standard to which activities that make up a sub-task (element) are to be carried out.
Portfolio	The collection and documentation of evidence to prove competence against the standards.
Qualifications and Curriculum Authority (QCA)	The government body that approves vocational and competence-based qualifications.
Range Statements	Contexts within which elements are assessed.

Scottish Qualifications Authority (SQA)	The government body that approves vocational and competence-based qualifications.
Scottish Vocational Qualifications (SVQ)	A qualification based on industry standards, operating in Scotland.
Sector Skills Council (SSC)	A body responsible for drawing up the industry standards.
Standard (of competence)	Drawn up by the NTO and including units, elements, performance criteria, range statements and underpinning knowledge and understanding.
Underpinning Knowledge and Understanding	The essential knowledge required to perform an element of competence.
Unit (of competence)	Major task(s) or function of a job/role. A unit can be individually certificated and is made up of elements.
V1	Verifier qualification, *Internally Verify Assessment Practice*.
V2	Verifier qualification, *Externally Verify Assessment Practice*.

Use the notes pages overleaf to record any additional terms you will find helpful.

Notes _____

Notes _____

Mission Statement

Our Vision

To have high-quality coaches and coaching interactions operating at every level within sport, contributing to an increase in participation, enjoyment and success in sport

Better coaches…better coaching…better sport
…more and better participants

Key components will be:

 a UK Coaching Certificate recognised as world leading in the qualification and continuous professional development of coaches

 a fit-for-purpose coaching workforce from grass roots to high performance across the UK, with the capacity, capability and quality to provide a sustained increase in sports participation and success in sports performance

 a high-quality coaching workforce with a culture of innovation and continuous professional development, with ethical values

 volunteer coaches, valued and nurtured, working alongside a career structure of professional coaches at community, club and performance levels of sport

 a coaching workforce that is representative of the local community in which it operates and the population

 a coaching workforce with the appropriate skills to use sport as a tool to support health, education and social inclusion objectives

Our Purpose

To lead the development of high-quality coaches via the provision of innovative products, services and expert guidance who are fit for purpose and readily available (right place, right time) to increase participation, performance and enjoyment in sport.